Making It in the Music Industry

Stuart A. Kallen

San Diego, CA

Printed in the United States

For more information, contact:
ReferencePoint Press, Inc.
PO Box 27779
San Diego, CA 92198
www.ReferencePointPress.com

LIBRARY OF CONGRESS CATALOGING-IN-PUBLICATION DATA

Names: Kallen, Stuart A., 1955- author.
Title: Making it in the music industry / by Stuart A. Kallen.
Description: San Diego, CA : ReferencePoint Press, 2026. | Includes bibliographical references and index.
Identifiers: LCCN 2025008433 (print) | LCCN 2025008434 (ebook) | ISBN 9781678210908 (library binding) | ISBN 9781678210915 (ebook)
Subjects: LCSH: Music trade--Vocational guidance--Juvenile literature. | Music--Vocational guidance--Juvenile literature.
Classification: LCC ML3795 .K16 2025 (print) | LCC ML3795 (ebook) | DDC 780.23--dc23/eng/20250304
LC record available at https://lccn.loc.gov/2025008433
LC ebook record available at https://lccn.loc.gov/2025008434

CONTENTS

Stepping Stones to Success

Norman Harris grew up during the 1960s playing rock and roll on an electric organ. Like countless other teens of that era, Harris dreamed of becoming a famous rock star in a chart-topping band like the Beatles or the Rolling Stones. Harris moved from Miami to Los Angeles to pursue his vision, but he quickly ran into reality. Harris found that he was just one of thousands of talented young musicians in Los Angeles trying to become the next big thing.

By the early 1970s, Harris was married, with a growing family and struggling to pay bills. But he had an idea that changed the course of his life. At the time the back pages of every major newspaper featured ads placed by people selling various items. Harris noticed that some people were selling high-quality, older guitars for low prices. He started buying some of these highly desirable guitars and selling them at a profit to various musicians he worked with. Word of Harris's vintage guitars spread throughout the Los Angeles music community. By 1975 Harris was buying and selling so many guitars that he was able to open a store, Norman's Rare Guitars, in Tarzana, California.

Norman's Rare Guitars grew into a destination for A-list musicians looking for rare or unusual instruments. By 2025 the seventy-five-year-old Harris was a major force in the music industry. He is credited with single-handedly launching the vintage guitar market, which is bigger than ever as older guitars increase in value.

Harris's life story was featured in a 2024 Netflix documentary, *Norman's Rare Guitars*. The film showed that a musician's dreams can take a detour that leads to another kind of success. Harris never became a rock star, but he is personal friends with dozens who achieved stardom. And his business has been wildly successful. As Harris said in 2019, "I realized I could make a few bucks buying and selling guitars. So that's what I started doing as my Plan B, and then Plan B became Plan A."[1]

Never Stop Dreaming

Harris's store attracts wealthy collectors who can afford to pay tens of thousands of dollars for guitars made during the mid-twentieth century. But the store also draws in teens eager to perform on the shop's YouTube channel, which has over 615,000 subscribers. Sometimes a young guitarist's performance will go viral. When eleven-year-old Saxon Weiss played a smooth jazz solo on a vintage Gibson guitar in 2023, the video racked up nearly two hundred thousand views.

Countless musicians hope to emulate Weiss's success. They write songs, play music, and upload performances to social media sites. Many dream of tapping their talents to become music superstars. Only a small percentage of musicians make music on a professional level, let alone the stratospheric heights achieved by megastars like Taylor Swift, Morgan Wallen, or Doja Cat. But earning a living as a musician is an attainable goal. Rich Redmond, who plays drums for country luminary Jason Aldean, describes the type of person who makes it in the country music capital of Nashville, Tennessee: "Most successful people achieve their dreams because they never take their eyes off the top of that pyramid. . . . It could happen in the first five minutes of arriving in Nashville, or it could take five or ten or fifteen years."[2]

"Most successful people achieve their dreams because they never take their eyes off the top of that pyramid. . . . It could happen in . . . five minutes . . . or it could take five or ten or fifteen years."[2]

—Rich Redmond, drummer

Rich Redmond (pictured) plays drums for country luminary Jason Aldean. As a youth, he spent countless hours practicing when he would rather have been riding his skateboard.

Redmond's path to a steady gig began when he was eight. He took drum lessons and, as he grew older, attended music workshops. He spent countless hours practicing when he would rather have been riding his skateboard. When he was older, he joined his high school's jazz band, symphonic band, and marching band. Redmond studied the moves of drummers he saw on music videos and went to college to get a degree in music.

Redmond's road map to success is old school; he never strived to become an internet star. He moved to Nashville and started at the bottom, playing local gigs for little money. Aldean heard Redmond playing in a bar and hired him to play drums in his band.

Redmond's methods are still followed by hundreds who move to music industry capitals like Nashville, Los Angeles, and New York City. But dozens of superstars, including Post Malone, Lizzo,

Lil Nas X, and Billie Eilish launched their careers without leaving home. They uploaded their songs to the music streaming service SoundCloud and utilized the power of video to attract likes and shares on sites such as YouTube, Instagram, and TikTok. After gaining a significant number of fans on social media, these stars attracted the attention of music industry insiders who offered them recording contracts. While stars follow their own recipes for success, Redmond's words ring true for anyone hoping to become a music superstar: "Success is waiting at the top, but there are many steps to reach that dream. . . . You must remain committed no matter what."[3]

CHAPTER ONE

Music Industry Players

When Jon-Carlo Manzo attended New York University (NYU) during the late 2010s, he majored in English. But Manzo's love for music led him to join NYU's program board, a student-run organization that plans events, including dances and concerts. Manzo says he did not initially know much about the music industry, but he learned a lot from working with other students: "They were all so much more involved and smarter than me, because those kids had been doing things when they were in high school, going to NYU's music-business-program summer camp and things like that."[4]

Program board meetings were an educational experience for Manzo. Board members often discussed booking as many as thirty different bands. Manzo wrote everything down and spent time after meetings researching the bands and learning about the record labels that released their music. As a member of the program board, Manzo worked with many people in the music business, including booking agents, publicists, venue managers, and others. Manzo also visited live-music venues, where he observed audiences to see what types of music people found most exciting.

After graduating in 2021, Manzo moved to Chicago, where he interned at a local record label called Fire Talk. His internship led him to a job at Pitch Perfect PR, a public relations (PR) firm that represents indie bands. PR specialists use social media to publicize their clients. They post videos and photos and monitor the postings to ensure their effectiveness in reaching targeted audiences. PR specialists provide an important link between artists, their music, and the public. Manzo said the job exposed him to many different sides of the music industry: "I started as just an admin assistant. I was just updating press reports and writing press releases for people. Now I'm veering into publicist territory with doing tour press and working on a bunch of artists that I've been a fan of for so long. I also helped with bringing in new clients to the company, because I have a pretty wide network."[5]

The Top of the Pyramid

PR specialists like Manzo are among many professionals who work in the music industry. And music is big business. The Recording Industry Association of America says the music industry supported nearly 2.5 million people while generating more than $170 billion in 2023.

To understand how the music industry works, it is helpful to think of it as a pyramid. Major record labels, which have been in business for decades, occupy the very top of the pyramid. Many musical artists dream of signing a contract with a record label, which indicates to the world that they have found success in the music business. Record labels sign artists, produce albums, fund ad campaigns, get music played on radio stations, and monetize music in a variety of ways. While most music is streamed or downloaded, some labels continue to manufacture physical compact discs (CDs) and vinyl records.

Lower on the pyramid are many small independent record labels, known as indies. These labels were often founded to focus on niche musical styles. Island Records, for example, found success promoting reggae music in the 1970s; it later went on to sign more mainstream pop music acts, including Florence + The Machine and Demi Lovato.

Indie labels usually offer artists the creative freedom to produce the music that inspires them. But indies cannot provide artists with

To understand how the music industry works, it is helpful to think of it as a pyramid. Major record labels, like Universal Music Group, occupy the very top of the pyramid.

the kinds of resources offered by the major labels known as the Big Three: Universal Music Group, Sony Music Entertainment, and Warner Music Group. Dan Rys, a senior writer at music industry magazine *Billboard*, explains why the Big Three record labels dominate the industry: "It's really important to focus on the fact that they have massive marketing and publicity muscle. They are the ones who are able to put a billboard up in Los Angeles. They're the ones who can get you placement on streaming services."[6] As Rys points out, streaming services—which are the main profit drivers for record labels—play an important role in the music industry. Digital music accounted for more than two-thirds of the music industry's gross revenue in 2023; over 667 million people subscribed to paid streaming services such as Spotify, Apple Music, and others.

"[The Big Three record labels] have massive marketing and publicity muscle. They are the ones who are able to put a billboard up in Los Angeles. They're the ones who can get you placement on streaming services."[6]

—Dan Rys, music writer

Signing and Recording Artists

When an artist signs a contract to be represented by a record label, it is often done at the behest of an artist and repertoire (A&R) director, a professional whose job focuses on discovering and developing new acts. A&R directors understand the music market, know what appeals to the public, and are directly responsible for much of the music people hear on a daily basis. Taylor Lindsey, an A&R director at Sony Music, explains what her company looks for in a new artist: "We really want to focus on signing people that are going to have a sustainable career. We don't want someone that is just going to be a one hit wonder. . . . We want to find the next thing, the next curve of radio, the next thing that excites listeners, the next evolution of the sound."[7]

> **"We want to find the next thing, the next curve of radio, the next thing that excites listeners, the next evolution of the sound."[7]**
>
> —Taylor Lindsey, A&R director at Sony Music

A&R directors oversee budgets, approve promotional photos and music videos, and work to build an artist's brand. They often pick potential hits out of dozens of songs presented to them by songwriters and music publishers. One of the most important roles for an A&R director is connecting an artist to a music producer who will oversee the recording process.

Music producers work with artists, studio musicians, and others to shape songs and bring them to life in a recording studio. Most producers are skilled musicians who use their knowledge of music and musical trends to produce sounds that will resonate with the public. Producers work closely with recording engineers, who understand the technical aspects of recording, including the use of electronic equipment, recording software, and computers.

Music journalist David Mellor explains the importance of choosing the right producer: "The producer can potentially make or break the record. . . . If a producer has a history of success with guitar orientated bands, then it would be a safe option to choose him to produce [a] newly signed guitar band. If a producer has had dance floor success, then he could be exactly right for [a] new solo artist."[8]

Music Publishers and Song Pluggers

When a professional songwriter writes a song, it is usually turned over to a music publisher upon completion. Music publishers ensure that the songwriters get paid for their creations. As guitarist and songwriter Johnny Garcia explains, "If you're a songwriter, you have to be published. Just like a book, there has to be a publisher or you can't sell it. A song cannot be put out there either [for] airplay, on a record, or on a jukebox without it being published." When songs are "put out there," the publisher ensures that the artist receives royalties—a percentage of the money the song earns.

Music publishers help artists earn royalties by promoting songs to artist and repertoire directors, music producers, and others. This work, called pitching a song, is often done by a song plugger. These individuals, sometimes referred to as musical matchmakers, are often industry veterans with many contacts. Pluggers understand which songs might be hits and which artists would best perform a song. Song pluggers also pitch songs to television producers, filmmakers, and ad agencies that might use a song for an advertisement.

Quoted in Rich Redmond and Jennifer Della'Zanna, *Making It in Country Music: An Insider's Look at the Industry*. Lanham, MD: Rowman & Littlefield, 2023, p. 80.

Managers and Agents

As the music industry pyramid widens from the top, a greater number of people can be found performing vital services. Successful recording artists hire financial advisers known as talent managers or business managers. These businesspeople are usually the closest person to an artist, outside of their family and friends. Managers help artists choose record deals, negotiate contracts, and take care of daily administrative tasks like paying bills. Business managers act as gatekeepers who limit public contact with the artist. They handle business-related phone calls, texts, and emails from record label executives, concert promoters, media representatives, and others. In return for their services, business managers are paid a percentage of an artist's revenues, usually around 10 percent.

Music agents, also referred to as booking agents or talent agents, have another role to play in the music business. They help musicians book and manage gigs. Music agents arrange, schedule, and promote individual concerts and tours, as well as booking press interviews and media appearances. They inspect and secure concert venues, negotiate performance fees, and sign contracts. Agents can also help developing artists connect with record labels.

Some agents are self-employed, but others work for talent agencies that handle most aspects of a performer's career. Alex Segal, who works for the InterTalent agency in London, says he has two clear goals for his clients: "Getting them noticed and getting them paid. How we get there, who we have to meet or call and what fires we have to put out along the way is part of a job that is a unique daily adventure. It's one of the reasons why I love my job."[9]

Music agents might represent up to twenty different acts, and they are always on the lookout for new talent. Some double as talent scouts, seeking out exceptional performers at theaters, clubs, and other entertainment venues. Scouts search through videos on YouTube and other social media platforms looking for people who have unique abilities. Talent scout Dan Dymtrow discovered

Business managers act as gatekeepers who limit access to the artist. They handle all communications from the record labels, promoters, media representatives, and others.

musical superstar Taylor Swift at the age of fourteen when she was playing her songs in a Nashville club. As Dymtrow said in 2004, "She blew me away with her talent, creativity, songwriting and personality."[10] Dymtrow had connections with Sony Music, which he used to get Swift a songwriting gig. This led to her recording her first album, *Taylor Swift*, in 2006.

Concert Promoters

Taylor Swift has had a major impact on the concert business. Her Eras Tour, which ran from March 2023 to December 2024 earned over $2 billion, making it the highest-grossing concert tour of all time. Swift has no problem packing stadiums with adoring fans. But she relies on a team of experienced music industry insiders who work behind the scenes to manage and promote her shows.

Concert promoter Louis Messina was the person in charge of running Swift's Eras Tour, as well as all of her other tours dating back to 2006. Messina, who began promoting concerts in 1973, also promotes shows for superstars such as George Strait, Ken-

Taylor Swift's Eras Tour earned over $2 billion, making it the highest-grossing concert tour ever. Swift relied on her concert promoter to manage and promote this record-breaking tour.

ny Chesney, Ed Sheeran, and Shawn Mendes. Although Messina has found great success, he says concert promotion is hard work:

> We don't stop working. We really don't. I mean when George is not working, we're still working on George. When Kenny's not working, we're still working on Kenny. Or we're still working on Ed or Taylor or Shawn, it's 24/7. If we're on tour this time with an artist, this tour is nothing but a stepping stone for the next tour and the tour after that. We're always planning what's next. Where do we go from here?. . . Our job is seven days a week and we don't stop, that's it in a nutshell.[11]

Messina has a large team and a track record that attracts top-name artists. And as he makes clear, the career of concert promoter is not for those who like to spend their days playing video games or scrolling through social media. Those who are new to concert promotion do most of the hard work themselves. According to concert promoter Robbie Kowal,

> We have broken it down to anywhere from sixty to eighty individual tasks to be done to run a successful show. Each one of these details is no more important than the others. For instance, there's getting the right artist and the right venue, making an offer to the artist, agreeing to a deal with the artist, booking support, getting the artwork done and approved, and building the marketing and advertising plan. . . . You have to do the hotels, ground transport, [obtain sound equipment], get them the schedule . . . all those production things.[12]

Kowal says basic problems, like failing to line up the proper sound equipment, can cause a show to be canceled.

Concert promoters who are less well-known than Kowal and Messina need to be risk-takers. They use their own money to pay for hotels, transportation, advertising, and equipment and venue rentals. Promoters must compensate artists, bands, staff members, sound and light engineers, and all others before they pay themselves. As Kowal says, "Small-scale concert promotion is the riskiest role in the entire business. Anybody can do it, but to build a sustainable business is very difficult."[13]

Hustle Is the Name of the Game

Legendary concert promoter Bill Graham once said, "We're not in the music business, we're in the people business."[14] While Graham was talking about concert promotion, the same could be said for many other jobs in the music industry. Most who work in the music industry, from publicists to promoters, are outgoing and sociable. They are motivated by a love of music and can connect on a personal level with artists and others in

The Skills of Audio Engineers

Beyoncé is one of the most famous recording artists in the world, and millions of people know her name. The same cannot be said about DJ Swivel, a Grammy-winning recording engineer who has worked on many of Beyoncé's songs. DJ Swivel has also helped other hitmakers—including Jay Z and Rihanna—achieve unique sounds on their records.

Recording engineers are often unknown to the public, but their work can be heard on nearly every record sold in the past century. They are professionally trained to record, mix, and reproduce sound. They deal with the technical and mechanical aspects of recording: handling microphones, amplifiers, mixing consoles, and computer recording equipment. Recording engineers set up a singer's microphone, place numerous mics around a drum kit, and plug guitars, keyboards, and other electronic instruments into a soundboard. They often consult with artists days or weeks before a recording session to determine their needs in the studio. Before a session, engineers set up all the equipment and work with musicians to achieve good instrumental and vocal sounds. During a recording session, engineers sometimes take part in the creative process, advising musicians on ways to generate new sounds.

the industry. But as drummer Rich Redmond writes, survival in the business also requires an almost single-minded focus on success: "[Anyone] with staying power will tell you that the music industry . . . requires a massive amount of dedication to properly navigate—and 'properly' is not clearly defined. . . . In all the ways the music industry has changed since its inception, the amount of hustling you have to do to make it has not. It's the name of the game that's for sure."[15]

"In all the ways the music industry has changed since its inception, the amount of hustling you have to do to make it has not. It's the name of the game that's for sure."[15]

—Rich Redmond, drummer

CHAPTER TWO

Getting in the Game

In 2024, pop singer Pink earned over $580 million with her Summer Carnival Tour, and folk-pop artist Ed Sheeran brought in over $5 million a night on his Mathematics Tour. With these eye-popping numbers, it is easy to understand why so many musical performers want to work as professional musicians. But those who dream of riding in limousines and flying to concerts in private jets should remember that most working musicians rarely earn large sums of money. For every Pink, there are thousands struggling to make their talent pay.

While not everyone can be the next pop superstar, it is possible to earn a living as a gigging musician. Playing a gig involves performing live at clubs, theaters, and other concert venues. Some gigging musicians get their songs on the radio or rack up likes and shares on social media. Most are not household names, but they get personal satisfaction by pursuing their creative dreams. As best-selling author Elizabeth Gilbert writes about performing, "A creative life is an amplified life. It's a bigger life, a happier life, an expanded life, and a hell of a lot more interesting life."[16]

Educate Yourself

A creative life might be interesting, but musicians need strong focus and commitment if they hope to reach the level of success obtained by Pink, Sheeran, and other superstars. And for most, this dedication to their craft starts at an early age. Sheeran, who was born in 1991, began singing in a church choir when he was

> **"I learned harmony, I learned how to sing in tune, I learned how to perform . . . [by] failing. Time and time again. . . . [I learned] everything from the failures. Success happens from failing hundreds of times."[17]**
>
> **—Ed Sheeran, pop singer**

only four years old. At age eleven, he learned how to play guitar and write songs. But Sheeran denies being blessed with amazing talent. He says that he struggled to develop his musical skills during his teen years: "[Between the ages of fourteen and eighteen] I learned harmony, I learned how to sing in tune, I learned how to perform, I learned how to do it in time . . . [by] failing. Time and time again. . . . [I learned] everything from the failures. Success happens from failing hundreds of times."[17]

Sheeran had to overcome several obstacles on his road to success. He was bullied for his severe stutter, which only disap-

Artist Ed Sheeran brought in over $5 million a night on his Mathematics Tour. With these eye-popping numbers, it is easy to understand why so many people want to be professional musicians.

peared when he sang. When he was sixteen, Sheeran auditioned for a television show called *Britannia High* but was turned down by the producers. But Sheeran's perseverance paid off in 2011 when his first single, "The A Team," became a top-ten hit in Australia, Japan, the United Kingdom, and elsewhere. While some in the media viewed Sheeran as an overnight success, he had years of diligent practice and hard work to thank for that success.

Those who hope to build a career like Sheeran's can get ahead of the competition by obtaining a formal musical education. Artists who can read and write music broaden their chances of success in the music industry. The universal language of musical notation allows artists to communicate their ideas to others and pursue creative avenues when composing. And it is a necessary talent for those seeking to play in classical or jazz orchestras or who plan to work as session musicians or backup musicians in a band.

Drummer Rich Redmond says his college years were the most productive of his life. He says he spent sixteen to eighteen hours a

The Power of Mixtapes

Most professional musicians have demonstration recordings, or demos, of their songs that are used to get gigs and promote their music. When three to seven songs are compiled in a demo it is often referred to as a mixtape. A mixtape can be released on social media sites for free to increase an artist's profile and attract attention from music industry insiders. Sometimes mixtapes can go viral and launch a career. Colombian-born singer-rapper Kali Uchis understood this. In 2023 Uchis's third studio album, *Red Moon Rising*, was a critically acclaimed success. But Uchis could pin her career breakthrough on her mixtape *Drunken Babble*. Released in 2013 with a mix of styles, including doo-wop, jazz, hip-hop, and reggae, the mixtape is offered as a free download on Uchis's SoundCloud account. The music captured the attention of stars, like A$AP Rocky, Diplo, and Snoop Dogg.

Uchis went on to release four top ten albums. But as she said in a 2014 interview, she was initially reluctant to put out her mixtape: "I was definitely hesitant [to put out *Drunken Babble*]. I was thinking, 'Maybe it's too real.' I'm literally just crying. . . . I didn't make it for people to hear. . . . [Then] I was just like 'Eh [screw] it.'"

Quoted in Briana Younger, "Kali Uchis: 'I'm an Artist in Every Sense of the Word,'" Bandwidth.fm, American University Radio, April 22, 2014. https://bandwidth.wamu.org.

Practice is essential for you to improve your skill as a musician. Being able to play slower, faster, louder, or softer as needed by artists or bandleaders, results in a massive skill set.

day practicing, studying, rehearsing, and playing gigs. He did this for six years as he worked to earn a master's degree in music. Redmond met and played with many highly skilled student musicians at college. This helped him master different musical genres, including funk, pop, rock, Latin, and jazz. As Redmond puts it, "Practice, practice, and more practice is essential for you to improve your skill while you're learning the academic and technical parts of the business in school. Combining knowledge with skill and practicing thousands of hours is how you get to bring that to the stage with other musicians. Being told to play slower, faster, louder, or softer by artists, bandleaders, and conductors results in a massive skill set."[18]

Learn the Business

Redmond knows many professional musicians who have college degrees that helped them find success. And those who take courses that focus on the financial, legal, and marketing aspects of the music business are a step ahead of others who do not. Music business programs teach artists to understand recording contracts, music publishing deals, and management agreements.

This ensures that musicians will be paid fairly while retaining ownership of their original music. A business education provides a strong background when negotiating with venue owners, record label executives, agents, and others.

Like any other business owner, gigging musicians also need to know how to manage money. Musicians must draw up detailed budgets for recording projects, live gigs, tours, and marketing. Following a budget ensures that there will be enough money for promotion, equipment rental, transportation, food, and accommodations. And musicians need to have enough money to pay themselves and band members while setting aside funds for obligations like taxes and music union dues where appropriate.

Musicians interested in building their business and technical skills have a number of options. Almost all universities offer music degrees; some, such as the Berklee College of Music in Boston or the Julliard School in New York City, specialize in music and performing. Musicians can also study at community colleges and technical institutes. And there is ample information online. Blogs, articles, group chats, and tutorial videos and websites cover nearly every aspect of planning a music career. Musicians can learn online how to write a band bio, contact an agent, read a recording contract, and copyright an original song. And tutorials cover nearly every aspect of the recording process, focusing on popular software programs such as Logic Pro, Ableton Live, and Pro Tools.

Build a Professional Network

Drummer and bass guitarist Isai Lugo knew enough about the recording process to earn a living as a freelance sound engineer in Corpus Christi, Texas. But Lugo wanted to move to Nashville and find work as a backup musician for a major country act. He knew that networking was the key to success, but he did not have many connections in the Nashville area. Lugo solved his problem by taking a job at a Nashville music store where the customers included musicians, producers, and other industry insiders. Lugo's networking helped him land a major touring gig as a drummer, which allowed him to quit his day job.

Build a Press Kit

When a booker, A&R director, or journalist expresses interest in a musical act, one of the first things they want to see is an electronic press kit (EPK). An EPK is an assortment of text, photos, artwork, videos, and music files that best represent the artist. The text portion of an EPK is usually a one-paragraph biography with a few sentences that describe the artist's music, motivation, and inspiration and a brief description of standout gigs or other memorable moments.

Photos included in an EPK need to be high-quality shots that can be used in advertisements for the act. A portrait-style picture of the artist, called a headshot, should accompany performance photos. Photos should present the act as energetic and professional. A few video clips of memorable performances can also be included along with album artwork if available.

The music is obviously the most important part of an EPK. The press kit should contain links to music files on SoundCloud and Bandcamp and to sites such as YouTube, Instagram, TikTok, and X. If compiling an EPK seems daunting, there are a number of websites with templates that can make the process easier.

Networking is fundamental to success in the music business, but it is not always easy. There are some basic rules that can make networking a little easier. Keep in mind that building a strong network takes time and patience. Most industry insiders built up their networks over years, not months. Most often, these networks were created one handshake at a time at music festivals, industry conferences, workshops, and seminars. And pursuing connections at these venues can be an educational experience. According to Mathilde Neu, a music business communications expert, "Engaging with experienced professionals, managers, producers, and industry insiders gives you access to a wealth of knowledge. . . . You'll gain confidence from these [connections]—resulting in better decision-making, performance, and long-term career success and sustainability."[19]

Networking can be easier for musicians who attend jam sessions and open mic nights. Playing music with other people is a great way to make new friends who might offer good advice—and industry connections. Open mic nights in entertainment capitals like New York, Los Angeles, and Nashville are often attended by talent

> **"If you network with booking agents, venue owners, and event organizers, you'll have a greater chance of securing gigs and festival performances. . . . Remember, word-of-mouth referrals and personal connections go a long way."[20]**
>
> —Mathilde Neu, music business communications expert

scouts, bookers, promoters, and A&R directors. As Neu writes, "If you network with booking agents, venue owners, and event organizers, you'll have a greater chance of securing gigs and festival performances. . . . Remember, word-of-mouth referrals and personal connections go a long way because professionals trust the referrals of others."[20]

In addition to gaining knowledge of the industry, networking can boost a career in other ways. Connecting with songwriters, music producers, studio engineers, and other musicians can lead to new collaborations. Working with others can help boost an artist's skills while opening doors to new creative possibilities. Singer-songwriter Dua Lipa is known for her successful collaborations with other artists. Early in her career, Lipa was a featured singer on Sean Paul's 2016 Jamaican dancehall hit "No Lie." The song became a top-ten hit in ten countries, including the United Kingdom. The video that featured the duo singing together went viral, which helped Lipa tap into a new audience. In the years that followed, Lipa collaborated with Miley Cyrus, Megan Thee Stallion, the K-pop band Twice, and even Italian opera singer Andrea Bocelli.

Build a Brand Online

Face-to-face contacts are best for building relationships, but social media can also be a useful networking tool. Musicians who wish to attract the attention of bookers, A&R directors, and others need to create a brand and promote it on a personal website. Many musicians do not like to think of themselves or their music as a brand—a term commonly associated with the marketing of food, cars, and other products. But establishing a unique brand with personal photos, stories, and behind-the-scenes snapshots can help attract notice from music industry insiders. Many musicians draw attention with a mixtape, which is a self-produced album released free of charge to attract publicity. A mixtape can be posted on social me-

Social media is a useful networking tool. Musicians who wish to attract the attention of bookers, record labels, and others need to promote their brand on digital media.

dia, which can help an unknown musician launch a career as their music gets shared and retweeted to a wider audience. Music industry consultant Kari Estrin explains why a good digital presence is essential: "[Record labels] rely on the artist to . . . come to them with a bevy of fans and resources already established in order for the label to take them on. . . . Artists themselves have to become savvy with social and digital media, while continuing to find ways to break through without label support."[21]

> **"[Record labels] rely on the artist to . . . come to them with a bevy of fans and resources already established in order for the label to take them on."[21]**
>
> **—Kari Estrin, music industry consultant**

Country music superstar Kane Brown was able to launch a successful career by breaking through online. Brown is one of the best-selling country music artists of the twenty-first century. His 2024 single "I Can Feel It" was his tenth number-one hit and his In the Air tour was selling out venues all over the world. But in 2014 Brown was an unknown musician when he recorded a video of himself strumming the guitar and singing George Strait's "Check Yes or No." Although the sound quality was poor, Brown's honey baritone voice and smooth country delivery shone through. The video went viral when it was posted to social media, quickly receiving over 7 million views.

Brown followed up his initial success with more homemade videos, playing songs by other popular country artists. He watched in amazement as his number of followers climbed to over 1 million. This led Brown to launch a Kickstarter campaign to finance production of the six-song extended play (EP) record *Closer*. When the EP was completed, Brown generated interest by posting short song clips with iTunes links, which prompted fans to purchase the songs.

Brown's online success led to a record contract with the RCA Nashville label in 2016. He went on to create more than a dozen top-ten singles on country music charts. Brown also won awards from the Academy of Country Music, People's Choice, and iHeartRadio. His 2023 Entertainer of the Year nomination by the Academy of Country Music was a testament to his rise from a social media star to one of country music's most popular global entertainers.

Keep Your Expectations in Check

Some of the world's most popular musical artists followed Brown's path to the top, including Justin Bieber, Doja Cat, Shawn Mendes, the Weeknd, and Lil Nas X. Like Brown, most attracted notice because they filled a niche; they specialized in a specific type of music or created a unique sound that helped them stand out in a crowded field.

For every artist that launched a successful career on social media, there are thousands who never attract notice. That makes it important for untested musicians to manage their expectations. Talent does not always rise to the top, and the life of a gigging musician can be difficult. But those who set realistic goals and build their talents, technical skills, and audience base can find joy in creating music and presenting it to others. Enthusiasm for music goes a long way when struggling with the realities of the music business. As Redmond writes, "One thing you always have control over in this business is your attitude. . . . What's kept me on track . . . has been a positive attitude and an unwavering belief that I could be a staple of this community."[22]

Making Money From Music

In 1989, when Heather Morgan was just five years old, she began stringing words together to form song lyrics. By the time she was in her late twenties, Morgan was working as a staff writer for the music publishing division of a major Nashville music label. As a songwriter, Morgan dedicates her life to telling compelling musical stories. She writes melodies, rhythms, and musical "hooks" meant to grab the attention of the listener. Some of Morgan's lyrics are simple and to the point; others contain sweeping cinematic poetry drawn from her personal experiences. Morgan's creative inspiration has brought her great financial rewards. She has written hit songs for country superstars like Brett Eldredge, Dierks Bentley, Keith Urban, and Maddie & Tae.

Songwriters like Morgan can sometimes feel as if they are being pulled in two directions at once. On one hand, they want to focus on their love of music and the inspiration and exhilaration it provides. On the other hand, they want to earn enough money to finance their musical careers. As songwriter Jason Blume explains, "Creative people are required to wear two proverbial hats—one as the creator and one as the business person or marketer of what we create. I sometimes say we need to have the tender, open heart of an artist and the [tough] skin of an armadillo."[23]

"Creative people are required to wear two proverbial hats—one as the creator and one as the business person or marketer of what we create."[23]

—Jason Blume, songwriter

It can be a challenge to harmonize creative inspiration with the grind of the music business. And sometimes the struggle

Songwriters want to focus on their inspiration and love of music. But they also have to consider music listeners' tastes if they want to be financially successful as well.

of trying to be a musical entrepreneur can overshadow the joy of playing. But there are a number of revenue streams that can be tapped to help an artist build and sustain a career in music.

Writing Songs

Blume spent more than a decade as a staff writer in Nashville. Contrary to what the term *staff writer* implies, songwriters like Blume do not earn a living as employees of music publishing companies. Staff writers sign exclusive songwriting contracts granting music publishers the right to sell their songs. In return for this commitment, staff writers receive royalties—a percentage of the money generated by sales of the songs they write.

Contracts for staff writers contain what is called a delivery requirement; this spells out the specific number of songs the writer must produce annually. The delivery requirement is usually ten to fifteen songs. If a staff writer cowrites with another staff writer, each songwriter receives half a credit toward the delivery requirement. Since staff writers often collaborate with others, they usually write anywhere from fifteen to thirty songs per year to meet their delivery requirements.

Songwriters often record simple demos that consist of a single instrument and a vocal sung by the songwriter. If the song is more complex, a demo might include a band or even a full orchestra. However, music publishers require songwriters to pay for the studio time and the backing musicians used on a demo. This can cost thousands of dollars, so most staff writers keep things simple. After a demo is completed, an A&R manager will try to attract interest from recording artists, producers, and other song buyers.

Taylor Swift famously began her career as a songwriter for a publishing company. And she is one of many superstars who started out writing for others. Before he was famous, Bruno Mars had a music publishing deal crafting songs for stars such as Snoop Dogg, Alicia Keys, Adele, and CeeLo Green. When Lady Gaga was a struggling artist, she was able to land a publishing deal with Sony writing songs for Britney Spears, Adam Lambert, and the Pussycat Dolls. Other staff writers who became major stars include Frank Ocean, Kasey Musgraves, and Sia.

There are many benefits to being a staff writer, and numerous people compete for a small number of openings. This leaves many dedicated songwriters to work as freelancers. Whether a songwriter is a freelancer or a staff writer, earning a living from writing songs is difficult. Those who write big hits can make a significant amount of money, especially if the song is used in a television show, movie, or commercial. But royalty rates for most songwriters only amount to a few cents per stream or download.

Music Distribution Services

Despite the hurdles, songwriters and other musicians can earn money by creatively marketing their talents. Some eliminate the need to work with music publishers by selling their music directly from personal websites. This method of monetizing music allows the songwriter to keep all of the money the song generates. Selling from a personal website also allows an artist to market other merchandise, such as T-shirts, coffee cups, and posters.

Independent artists who seek a wider audience can sell their music in digital music stores such as Apple, Spotify, Pandora, and Amazon. The simplest way to achieve this is to use a digital music distribution service. In 2025 there were more than a dozen of these platforms, including DistroKid, CD Baby, LANDR, and TuneCore. They all operate the same way. Digital music distribution services charge customers around twenty-five dollars annually to place songs with over 250 digital stores and streaming services worldwide. There is no limit to the number of songs an artist can upload, and the artist retains complete ownership of the music. The services collect and pay the artist all proceeds generated by a song. This frees musicians from having to keep track of money coming in from various sources. The services also offer tools artists can use to update their online profiles, interact with fans, promote tracks on social media, and analyze a song's performance. Some also distribute music videos. The singer-songwriter known as BØRNS, explains why he likes distributing his songs through DistroKid: "It's very user-friendly, and it feels

Musicians who seek a wider audience can sell their music in digital music stores using a digital music distribution service like DistroKid.

Marketing Merch

Musicians can spend a year or more writing and recording a twelve-song album. When it is sold from an online music store such as iTunes, the musicians make around six dollars per download. When those same musicians sell a T-shirt bearing their name for thirty dollars, they make a profit of more than twenty dollars. This simple math explains why so many musicians concentrate on selling branded merchandise, or merch, for short.

Merchandise is a great way to brand an artist and help them stand out from the competition. Merch can be sold at concerts, from personal websites, and from artist storefronts on Amazon. Those who sell merch online often use what is called a drop-shipping service. A drop-shipping company makes, packs, and ships merchandise on demand (only when it is ordered). This means artists do not have to pay up front for items that might never be sold. The alt-pop artist RAIGN designs her own merch and lets a drop shipper handle the rest: "There's nothing to lose! It's a really fantastic way to design all the merch your heart desires *and* get it shipped to an international fanbase. I did a lot of research and couldn't find another way to have complete control over the design process."

Quoted in Sarah Reilly, "More than Music: Artist RAIGN on Making Original Merch," Printful, April 19, 2022. www.printful.com.

very simple. . . . It's important to me moving forward that I'm able to own the music that I create so I can sustain myself as an independent musician. DistroKid has made it very clear that they also believe that's true, and that makes me feel very supported and comfortable working with them."[24]

As with any online service, users need to carefully read the terms presented by digital distribution services. Some have hidden fees or take a cut of the user's royalties. There are numerous articles, tutorials, and reviews of these services online, and those who take the time to research their options can expect a better outcome.

Start Performing Live

Using a digital distribution service is a relatively new way to profit from music. But many experienced musicians make money the old-fashioned way: they play live at venues that range from coffeehouses to concert halls. Finding and playing live gigs is not always easy, but people still pay for the experience of hearing live music. And interacting with audiences can be a gratifying experience that also carries financial rewards.

Most beginners in the music business do not earn money from their first live gigs. But playing live is fun and also a necessary step for those who hope to build audiences and advance their careers. Signing up for choir at school or a church is a great way to gain experience. Singing in a choir is an opportunity for vocalists to learn to sing in harmony and practice good techniques like pitch accuracy and breath control. Some of the biggest stars, including Whitney Houston, John Legend, Katy Perry, and GloRilla made their first public appearances in their church choirs.

Artists who are not interested in joining choirs can get live performance experience at open mic nights. As the term implies, open mic events are open to anyone, including musicians, stand-up comics, and poets of any skill level. Times, locations, and signup details for open mic nights can be found on the pages of local music groups on Facebook and other sites. Some apps, including Eventbrite and Yelp, list open mic nights.

Open mics are most often hosted by experienced musicians who might play a few songs and act as a backup musician for other acts. There is usually a sign-up sheet, and musicians who sign up early get to play earlier in the evening. Performers generally can play two to five songs depending on the number of other acts that have signed up. Most open mic stages have microphones, but musicians need to bring their own instruments and whatever other musical equipment they might need.

Open mic nights are good places to try out new material and gauge the audience reaction. And they are great places to network; musicians can meet collaborators and, sometimes, industry insiders who attend open mic nights to look for new talent.

Get Paid to Play

Open mic nights might be fun and easy, but these gigs do not pay. Musicians who want to earn money playing live need to book shows at local bars, breweries, clubs, and similar venues. (Places

Musicians who want to earn money playing live need to book shows at local bars, breweries, clubs, and similar venues. There are online tools to help find opportunities.

that serve liquor generally require musicians to be at least twenty-one years old.) Musicians who have websites and electronic press kits with music clips, photos, and videos can find gig opportunities online using sites such as ReverbNation, Sonicbids, and GigSalad. These sites allow users to create an artist profile, upload a few songs, and access gig information for free. They charge monthly fees to provide other services, like uploading unlimited videos and sending press kits to contacts.

Online booking sites are helpful to those looking to be hired for private events such as weddings and corporate gigs. These are some of the best-paying gigs available. However, private events are not usually places where musicians can show off their raucous punk, hip-hop, or heavy metal skills. Most event planners want musicians who can play softly in the background while people are having cocktails and dining. Musicians are often required to play familiar oldies and popular new songs for after-dinner dancing.

Do It Yourself

The competition for gigs at traditional venues can be fierce. This leaves some musicians to promote themselves at house concerts, which are shows held in homes, art galleries, barns, parks, warehouses, community centers, school and church auditoriums, or any other community space that can hold a crowd.

There are challenges to do-it-yourself (DIY) concerts: artists need to promote the event, sell tickets, and take care of all the other planning that goes into hosting a live show. But there are online services to help those interested in planning house concerts. The Side Door website, for example, connects artists with people who are willing to host house concerts. The hosts post profiles and often help artists sell tickets and manage shows. Side Door cofounder Laura Simpson explains the basic benefits of her service: "Doing a show in an alternative space allows you to choose the space to suit the performance. Does it need to be super quiet? Try an art gallery. Do you sing about nature? Try a park. Do you want to have cute animals around? Try a house with a dog or a barn."[25]

Some musicians prefer to host DIY concerts without leaving the comfort of their homes. This leads them to organize online concerts. The singer-songwriter Sereda, who performs using a single name, is very familiar with online concerts. Sereda, who lives in Los Angeles, attempted to follow the traditional path to the top. She recorded demos, met with agents and record label executives, and played low-paying bar gigs in hopes of gaining exposure. Nothing seemed to work until a friend introduced her to the live stream gaming platform Twitch. The site is known for professional gamers who earn money showing off their game-playing skills to followers. Sereda is not a gamer, but she thought her songwriting skills might attract some fans on Twitch. In 2020 she began live streaming herself while she wrote and performed new songs. Within a year she had more than two hundred thousand followers and was earning $4,500 a month from donations, subscriptions, and money paid by

"Doing a show in an alternative space allows you to choose the space to suit the performance. Does it need to be super quiet? Try an art gallery. Do you sing about nature? Try a park."[25]

—Laura Simpson, cofounder of Side Door house concert service

Make Music for Radio Playlists

Some of the most popular playlists on digital radio stations feature instrumental music created for people who are studying, exercising, and relaxing. Spotify has over 150 of these playlists, including "Ambient Relaxation," "Deep Focus," and "Morning Stretch." Many musicians who create mood music for these instrumental playlists are employed by production companies that pay a one-time fee for each track. This arrangement is called a work-for-hire gig. Musicians who take on work-for-hire gigs often do not use their real names because they do not want to be publicly associated with music defined as playlist filler. An unnamed jazz musician who spoke to journalist Liz Pelly said the work is not glamorous:

> For most of this stuff, I just write out [music] charts while lying on my back on the couch. And then once we have a critical mass, they organize a [recording] session and we play them. And it's usually just like, one take, one take, one take, one take. You knock out like fifteen in an hour or two. . . . There are so many things in music that you treat as grunt work. This kind of felt like the same category as wedding gigs or corporate gigs.

Quoted in Liz Pelly, "The Ghost in the Machine," *Harper's*, January 2025. https://harpers.org.

Twitch for ads viewed on her page. Sereda says, "The support that I have received from people who have come to find my channel on Twitch is something I've never experienced. Here I am, an independent artist with no record label, no publishing deal, no manager, no help from anybody, literally just me and this platform, Twitch."[26]

Sereda was still live streaming on Twitch in 2025. She cross-promotes her music on other social platforms, including Discord, Snapchat, and YouTube. Sereda might not be a wealthy celebrity, but her creative marketing skills allow her to live her best life writing songs and recording music. That makes Sereda a success, as the word is defined by iconic singer-songwriter Bob Dylan: "[A person] is a success if he gets up in the morning and gets to bed at night, and in between he does what he wants to do."[27] While the music industry is in constant flux, there are many avenues to success. Musicians who get to do what they want to do every day are only limited by their imaginations.

CHAPTER FOUR

How Stars Are Born

When the rap superstar Kendrick Lamar headlined the Super Bowl halftime show in 2025, his explosive performance was one for the record books. Lamar was the first solo rapper to perform at a Super Bowl and, according to Apple Music, more than 133 million people tuned in to watch his career-spanning set. This broke the record for the most-watched halftime performance in Super Bowl history.

Lamar was undoubtedly at the peak of his already successful career in 2025. But his musical influences can be traced to the poverty and violence he experienced as a child growing up in Compton, California, during the 1990s. At the time Compton, a small city located south of downtown Los Angeles, was often referred to as a war zone. Lamar witnessed his first murder at age five when a teen drug dealer was gunned down outside his apartment building. Several years later he saw another murder—this one at a local hamburger stand.

Life in Compton was not all bad. In 1995, when he was seven, Lamar watched two popular gangsta rappers, Dr. Dre and Tupac Shakur, shoot a video of the song "California Love" on a corner by his apartment. He decided then and there that he would become a rapper. There was just one problem with that plan: whenever Lamar got excited or fearful, he stuttered. But Lamar did not let the stutter hold him back, as he explained in 2014: "I put my energy into making music. That's how I get my thoughts out."[28]

> **"I put my energy into making music. That's how I get my thoughts out."[28]**
>
> —Kendrick Lamar, hip-hop superstar

Lamar, who eventually stopped stuttering, was a straight A student who read the dictionary to find new and interesting words. Lamar's teachers encouraged him to study poetry, and he spent his free time filling notebooks with rap lyrics. Many lyrics were eyewitness accounts of home invasion robberies and people running from the police. As Lamar later recalled, "My uncles and all my cousins was doing it on a daily basis—shootouts, running in my momma house, trying to hide somewhere, selling dope. So for a while I thought that was how it was supposed to be, until I ventured out into other spaces and people didn't know about what was going on where I was from."[29]

Mixtape Emotions

The constant chaos and violence took an emotional toll on Lamar; he felt frustrated and angry. He channeled these feelings into the contents of his first mixtape, which he released in 2003 at the age of sixteen. Lamar used the stage name K-Dot on the mixtape.

Kendrick Lamar performed at the 2025 Super Bowl, breaking the record for the most-watched halftime performance in Super Bowl history.

Mixtapes are usually given away for free to attract publicity, and this one accomplished that goal. The songs grabbed the attention of Anthony "Top Dawg" Tiffith, a local record producer and manager of rap acts. Tiffith was astounded by the streetwise maturity displayed on the mixtape and could scarcely believe that the music was coming from such a young man. He was so enthralled with Lamar's complex rhymes that he founded an indie record label, Top Dawg Entertainment (TDE), solely to promote the young rapper.

When Tiffith founded TDE, he wrote a five-point plan to describe the core traits a successful rap star needed to possess: "Charisma, Substance, Lyrics, Uniqueness, and Work Ethic."[30] These words were written on a poster board hanging on the wall in the TDE studio, where Lamar created new songs for several years. Lamar's local fame continued to grow with the release of his third mixtape, *C4* (2009). The tracks were heavily influenced by rap superstar Lil Wayne, who Lamar had met on a video shoot. In 2010 Lamar had a career breakthrough with the mixtape *OD: Overly Dedicated*. The critically acclaimed mixtape helped establish Lamar as one of the most talented rappers in the West Coast hip-hop scene.

Green Day's Political Punk

Green Day might have been one of the most famous punk rock bands in the world when the Linda Lindas worked as its opening act in 2024. But when the supersonic band released its 1994 album *Dookie*, critics panned it for its unique blend of punk, rock, and pop. Hardcore fans derided the sound as too poppy, calling it mall punk. But Green Day had a fresh take on the sound, and *Dookie* went on to sell 20 million copies worldwide.

Green Day's follow-up albums did not sell as well. But the group reversed its fortunes with the 2004 album *American Idiot*, a rock opera that presents a scathing portrait of twenty-first century American life. The album sold over 14 million copies and produced five chart-topping singles, including the classic "Wake Me Up When September Ends." The album also inspired the 2010 Broadway play *American Idiot: The Musical*. Mixing cultural criticism and politics with music is tricky, and many musicians who try this do not succeed. But band songwriter Billie Joe Armstrong was able to express his beliefs in a way that built a foundation for Green Day's continuing success well into the 2020s.

Lamar went on to become one of the most successful rappers of all time. In 2018 he was awarded the Pulitzer Prize for Music. No rap or pop artist had ever received this prestigious award.

In 2025, the week before his Super Bowl appearance, Lamar won an astounding five Grammy Awards for his track "Not Like Us." By this time, Lamar was described as one of the most popular rappers of the twenty-first century. His achievements can be traced back to the five traits for success pinned on the wall during his early years. Throughout his career Lamar constantly exhibited the charisma, substance, lyrics, uniqueness, and work ethic that took him to the top.

The Linda Lindas Riot

During the 1990s, when Lamar began writing rap lyrics, he was among a growing number of young people who were expressing in music their dissatisfaction with society. In the Pacific Northwest, the feminist punk rock band Bikini Kill launched the riot grrrl movement with songs that addressed tough issues like domestic abuse, sexism, and racism.

The music of Bikini Kill continued to inspire many young musicians in the twenty-first century. That influence extended to a group of Los Angeles girls who formed the Linda Lindas in 2018. The Linda Lindas took its name from a Japanese film, *Linda, Linda, Linda*, about a group of high school girls who form a punk rock band. But at the time, only one member of the Linda Lindas, fourteen-year-old guitarist Bela Salaza, was high school age. Guitarist Lucia de la Garza was eleven; her sister who plays drums, Mila de la Garza, was eight. The group's bassist, Eloise Wong, a cousin to Lucia and Mila, was eleven.

The Linda Lindas first gig was in 2018 at an annual all-ages benefit, Save Music in Chinatown, which raises money for a local elementary school's music program. Despite the musicians' youth and inexperience, the band's raw energy impressed other musicians on the bill. Among those who were impressed was actor Amy Poehler, who helped the Linda Lindas land a gig as the opening act for Bikini Kill at the Hollywood Palladium in 2019.

The riot grrrl attitude of Bikini Kill struck a chord with Mila, who wrote the song "Racist, Sexist Boy" after a schoolmate made a bigoted comment to her. In 2021 the Linda Lindas played "Racist, Sexist Boy" at the TEENtastic Tuesday Event hosted by the Los Angeles Public Library. A video of the performance went viral, and a week later the band made its network television debut on *Jimmy Kimmel Live*. As Eloise later recalled, "Suddenly our email was flooded and we had a bunch of interviews and it was like, whoa, what is this? It's cool that [our] message resonated with so many

The young band the Linda Lindas have raw energy when they perform. This impressed actor Amy Poehler, who helped the band land a gig at the Hollywood Palladium.

people. . . . It's cool because it came from such an angry place and suddenly something so light came out of it."[31]

> "It's cool that message [of 'Racist, Sexist Boy'] resonated with so many people. . . . It's cool because it came from such an angry place and suddenly something so light came out of it."[31]
>
> —Eloise Wong, Linda Lindas bassist

The Linda Lindas landed a record contract and released its first album, the appropriately named *Growing Up*, in 2022. The band hit the big time the following year when it played at the twenty-second Coachella Valley Music and Arts Festival. Continuing its success in 2024, the Linda Lindas opened for the legendary rock group the Rolling Stones. Months later, the group played to packed stadiums as the opening act for another one of its influences, the iconic pop punk band Green Day. The young members of the Linda Lindas were warmly received by Green Day fans, many of whom were old enough to be their parents.

Not many teens have to focus on their homework after hanging out with Green Day's leader Billie Joe Armstrong, but the members of the Linda Lindas take it all in stride. As Lucia says, "We have good friends and understanding teachers. It's a little balancing act. . . . We're going to be done [with the tour] soon and we'll see what happens after that. But right now we enjoy both. We try to have fun with [the bands]. It's a little stressful, especially when we're on tour. We had to do school on tour, but it was worth it."[32]

The Linda Lindas dropped their second album, *No Obligation*, in 2024. Countless musicians dream of the type of success achieved by the Linda Lindas, but the band followed a path taken by many others. Band members were very ambitious from the beginning and spent many hours practicing together. The group played benefits, networked with other musicians, and recorded a video that went viral. The Linda Lindas also found a niche; there were very few schoolgirls forming punk rock bands during the late 2010s, even in Los Angeles. Lucia offered this advice to up-and-coming musicians: "You have to just go for it. It's easy to be scared of what other people think of you, but like, I think it's really important to try to place yourself around people that are just gonna lift you up"[33]

Chappell Roan, the Midwest Princess

Being surrounded by people who offer positive support is essential, as award-winning singer Chappell Roan understands. Her road to the top was rocky. But encouragement from the gay and trans community helped her push through some crushing disappointments she experienced on the way to building a successful career.

Roan was born Kayleigh Rose Amstutz in 1998. She began playing piano when she was ten years old, and by the time she was thirteen she was performing in her hometown of Willard, Missouri. Roan built up a digital presence by posting performance videos on

Singer Chappell Roan (center) said encouragement from the LGBTQ community helped her push through some crushing disappointments she experienced on the way to building a successful career.

YouTube. She auditioned for *America's Got Talent* when she was fourteen, but she was not invited to participate in the competition.

Undeterred, Roan continued to hone her talents, playing gigs around her hometown and in nearby Springfield. When she was seventeen she attended an arts education summer program at the Interlochen Arts Camp in Interlochen, Michigan. Roan said it was a life-changing experience: "[I'd] never met creative kids before that camp, and it changed my trajectory forever. I'd never been with other songwriters before in my life that were my age. . . . There were kids from all over the world there. It was just so inspiring."[34]

During her time at camp, Roan wrote the song "Die Young," which she uploaded to YouTube. The song attracted attention from several record labels. It seemed as if Roan's dreams were coming true; she was only seventeen when she signed a five-year recording contract with Atlantic Records. Roan moved to Hollywood and began writing and recording songs. Her debut EP *School Nights*, released in 2017, is a low-key album that features Roan singing and playing piano with little backing. She recorded several more songs, but like many artists, Roan struggled with her record label. Atlantic refused to release her new music; after five years, the label dropped her. In 2020, with money running out, she moved back in with her parents and got a job working at a drive-through coffee kiosk. Roan says that despite the set-backs, she believed in her music and refused to quit: "I would tell myself, 'just keep going, don't stop.'"[35]

Roan saved up money and moved back to Los Angeles in 2022. She focused on building a career as an independent artist while working a series of low-wage jobs. Roan's music took on a new sound with the single "Naked in Manhattan," which features bubbly synthesizers and disco dance beats. The video reveals why Roan calls herself a thrift store pop star. She is shown running around New York City in elaborate outfits pieced together from thrift store clothing. Roan, who takes her inspiration from drag performers, explained the DIY spirit in the video: "I learned how to do drag makeup and how to bedazzle and sew a little bit.

"I learned how to do drag makeup and how to bedazzle and sew a little bit. There were so many things I had to learn out of necessity, and that's what built this project."[36]

—Chappell Roan, singer-songwriter

There were so many things I had to learn out of necessity, and that's what built this project."[36]

In 2023 Roan released her debut studio album, *The Rise and Fall of a Midwest Princess*. She said the breakthrough album, which received nearly universal acclaim, was the "absolute opposite" of her EP: "I rose from the ashes of losing all my money and moving back in with my parents and working the drive-through—this beautiful project came to life from the deep pits of hell."[37] *The Rise and Fall of a Midwest Princess* sold over 1 million copies and reached number two on the US album charts. In 2025 Roan received six Grammy nominations and won the Best New Artist award.

The Revolutionary Style of Lil Wayne

Kendrick Lamar often praised Lil Wayne in interviews, calling him the world's greatest rapper. And if sales figures are any indication, the public backs Lamar's assessment. Between 1999 and 2025, Lil Wayne sold over 120 million records worldwide, making him one of the best-selling artists of all time.

Lil Wayne's iconic looks initially helped him stand out from the crowd. He was one of the earliest rappers to sport dreadlocks and multiple face tattoos, now a ubiquitous trend among rappers, including Post Malone, Lil Pump, and Travis Scott. But Lil Wayne's main claim to fame can be traced to his pioneering use of high-pitched, electronically altered vocals and his ability to freestyle, or improvise lyrics, like no one else. As journalist Sharmaine Johnson writes,

> His freestyle approach to creating music is a masterclass in spontaneity and raw creativity. Unlike many of his contemporaries, he often crafts his verses on the fly, bypassing written lyrics for a more instinctive flow. This technique allows him to deliver an unfiltered, authentic sound that truly connects with listeners. . . . This unique style has become a defining element of his legacy, setting a standard that other rappers have eagerly tried to follow.

Sharmaine Johnson, "13 Ways Lil Wayne Revolutionized Hip Hop," Revolt, November 7, 2024. www.revolt.tv.

Roan, who is lesbian, credits her success to the atmosphere of acceptance she provides at her concerts: "The shows are a way for me to give a safe space to queer people and to have fun and dress up. It feels like magic on stage. I'm literally getting teary-eyed because it's everything I ever wanted."[38]

Let the Music Flow

Roan is not the first musician to feel as if she rose from the pits. And there is little doubt that adversity can inspire great music, as Kendrick Lamar can attest. But the common thread that winds through most successful careers is the ability to let the music flow despite the setbacks that might be encountered. As Lamar put it in 2018, "My musicality has been driving me since I was four years old. It's just pieces of me, man, and how I execute it is the ultimate challenge."[39]

CHAPTER FIVE

Reality Check

The musical megastar Prince is widely considered to have been one of the greatest performers of his generation. As a songwriter, singer, and multi-instrumentalist, Prince incorporated funk, rhythm and blues, rock, jazz, hip-hop, and blues into a revolutionary new sound. Prince gained national attention with the 1980 album *Dirty Mind* and its 1981 follow-up *Controversy*. Prince was also a fashion trendsetter and filmmaker. His popularity continued to grow in 1984 after the release of the first of his five movies, the semiautobiographical *Purple Rain*. Prince's music influenced nearly every superstar who followed, including Beyoncé, Bruno Mars, H.E.R., Lady Gaga, Rihanna, and the Weeknd.

There is little doubt that Prince was a musical genius beloved by millions. But whatever his talents, he could still be outplayed by a predatory industry that has perfected ways to monetize music at the expense of artists. Prince was only nineteen when he signed a deal with Warner Records in 1978. Like many eager young artists, he committed a common error. Prince gave the record company control of his master recordings. A master recording is the original recording of a song. All other forms of that song, including vinyl records, cassettes, CDs, and digital files are copies of the master recording. Whoever owns the master recording has the legal right to profit from it in any way they choose. By signing over ownership of his master recordings, Prince granted Warner Records the right to collect a large percentage of the royalties generated by the songs.

During the 1990s, Prince began pursuing legal methods to regain the rights to his masters. He also took steps to sabotage his record deal with Warner Records.

When Prince released his fourteenth album in 1993, he gave it a name using an unpronounceable symbol. In this era, before the widespread use of digital graphics and the internet, the symbol was difficult to reproduce in ads and record reviews. Since no one could reference the name of the album, it sold around half as many copies as previous Prince albums.

Fighting Back

In the battle to regain ownership and artistic control of his music, Prince started using the unpronounceable symbol as his stage name. This became an international joke when the press began referring to him as "the Artist Formerly Known as Prince." As journalist Lisa Kay Davis writes, "Beleaguered by bad press, parodies and label retaliation, the Artist Formerly Known as Prince endured

Prince was only nineteen when he signed with Warner Records in 1978. Like many young artists, he made a common error by giving the record company control of his recordings.

> **"I don't own Prince's music. If you don't own your masters, your master owns you."[41]**
>
> —Prince, singer, songwriter, musician

public shaming in the name of musician rights. The more mature, experienced artist wanted out of the music contract he signed when he was only 19 years old and Warner [Records] was not budging."[40]

In 1995 Prince stirred up more controversy when he began performing with the word *slave* written on his cheek. Prince explained why he felt like a slave: "I don't own Prince's music. If you don't own your masters, your master owns you."[41]

Prince sold over 100 million records worldwide. This gave him the popularity and the power to go to battle against Warner Records, but his fight against the label lasted more than two decades. He finally regained control of his master recordings in 2014, two years before his death from a fentanyl overdose.

Prince's efforts have been cited by multiple other artists who fought to regain the rights to their masters, including Frank Ocean, Bruno Mars, and Taylor Swift. But most musicians signing traditional record deals are pressured by the labels to give away their master recording rights, and they often lack the financial resources to regain them.

Awful Record Contracts

Record labels take advantage of artists in many ways beyond gaining control of master recordings. As indie music consultant Circa writes, "Unless you are able to build a sizable following all by yourself, a major record label probably won't be interested in signing you. If they do, your contract will be awful."[42] Circa says that the average record deal contains page after page of dense legal language meant to baffle young artists. This was the situation encountered by rapper Megan Thee Stallion, who engaged in a yearslong battle against her record label, 1501 Certified Entertainment, over a contract she signed early in her career: "I didn't really know what was in my contract," she explained on Instagram Live in 2020. "I was young. I was, like, 20. . . . It's not that I literally

The Toll of Touring

A musician might dream of boarding a tour bus with a band and hitting the road to play a series of gigs. And playing live is often an exhilarating experience. But when the gig ends, the high from performing can dim as quickly as the stage lights. As most musicians know, touring can be stressful; living the life of a touring musician can lead to anxiety, depression, and substance abuse. Traveling musicians often live on fast food and have little time for self-care or exercise. And life on the road can take a toll on a musician's mental health. "I think I went through as many mental states as there are states in America," jokes one musician when discussing his time on the road. As he explains, "There's the high of being on stage, but the reality is mostly quite tedious—you're setting up all your gear, killing time before the gig, then packing it back down and getting back in the van, only to do it all again the next day."

Musicians seeking help for depression and other psychological problems can contact a number of organizations, including MusiCares, Music Minds Matter, and the Music Health Alliance.

Quoted in Musicians' Union, "Mental Health Support for Musicians," October 3, 2023. https://musiciansunion.org.uk.

didn't read [the contract], it's that I didn't understand some of the verbiage at the time. Now that I do, I just wanted it corrected."[43]

When Megan signed the contract in 2018, she was advised by a business manager who she later accused of secretly working for the record label. She did not understand that the contract gave the label an unusually high 60 percent of her recording revenue and 30 percent of touring and merchandising income. When Megan tried to renegotiate the contract two years later, the label blocked her from releasing her newest album, *Suga*. Megan waged a legal battle, claiming that the record label made $7 million while she was paid only $15,000. After a three-year fight, Megan was able to part ways with her label and was granted a multimillion-dollar payout.

When Megan Thee Stallion initially signed the record deal she was given a $10,000 advance, a fairly small amount by industry standards. Some new artists receive six-figure advances, which often prompts them to purchase expensive clothes, cars,

Before a single song is sold, an artist is charged for the use of a recording studio and engineers who work there. Musicians are also charged an array of administrative fees.

and instruments. But an advance is nothing more than a loan the record company makes against future earnings. The advance must be paid back through record sales, and the label makes this as difficult as possible. Before a single song is sold, an artist is charged for the use of a recording studio and salaries of the studio musicians and engineers who work there. Musicians are also charged an array of excessive fees for marketing, administration, tour support, radio promotion, and other activities. These fees can reach millions of dollars. As a result, many musicians never make money from their efforts, and they often end up owing the record label money—even if they

"Exploitative [record contracts] heavily favor record labels. . . . These contracts, presented as gateways to stardom, often strip artists of their creative freedom and control over their work."[44]

—Aryan, music business journalist

sell millions of records. As music business journalist Aryan writes, "Behind closed doors, exploitative agreements heavily favor record labels. . . . These contracts, presented as gateways to stardom, often strip artists of their creative freedom and control over their work. . . . The dreams of a promising career can quickly turn into a nightmare."[44]

Little Earnings From Streaming

Some artists choose to remain independent to avoid the pitfalls associated with record contracts. But indie artists have their own problems when releasing music, especially since most people listen to music on Spotify, Apple Music, YouTube Music, or other streaming platforms.

The exploding popularity of streaming has been beneficial for the music industry. In 2022 digital revenue accounted for nearly 90 percent of music industry profits. But streaming has not been profitable for most artists, particularly when compared to royalties earned before the invention of digital downloads and streaming. During the 1990s a popular artist might receive a 10 percent royalty on total record sales. If 1 million people bought a hit single, an artist could earn over $100,000.

Hundreds of artists in the days before streaming became millionaires by recording hit songs. That is not the case today. Spotify, the world's largest streaming service by a wide margin, pays an artist around $0.004 every time a song is streamed. Apple Music is slightly better, paying $0.007 per stream. That means that if 1 million people stream a song, Spotify pays the artist $4,000 and Apple pays $7,000.

Spotify announced a new policy for 2024 that has made it even more difficult for indie artists to monetize their music streams. Spotify said a track would have to reach a threshold of at least one thousand streams during a twelve-month period to qualify for royalty payments. Critics of this policy pointed out that 80 percent of the songs on Spotify, or more than 158 million tracks, do not reach this threshold.

In another twist, the money that would have gone to these artists will now be allocated to the artists who exceed the streaming threshold. Indie band member Greg Fuhs explains the impact of this policy, saying that Spotify claims

> that small indie artists won't miss this money—although I don't think Spotify asked any of us about this. . . . Furthermore, the ones that still do [reach the one-thousand-stream threshold] will now receive part of their streaming revenue from funds that used to go to lesser-known artists for their streams. . . . While the amount per artist may be small (although in some cases it could be substantial), it doesn't make Spotify's policy . . . any less wrong.[45]

Against the Odds

Streaming payouts might be low, but the glitz and glamour of the entertainment industry continues to attract countless musicians seeking fame and fortune. While many dream of stardom, only a small number succeed, according to a study by the music statistics platform Chartmetric.

In 2024 Chartmetric released its inaugural *Year in Music* report. The study tracked digital data on nearly 10 million musicians. Chartmetric used the information to rank artists by various measures of success across different streaming services, social media sites, and other platforms.

Chartmetric created six career-stage categories. The undiscovered category consists of artists who have yet to establish a consistent public presence. The next category, called developing, is filled by up-and-coming musicians who have a small online fan base. Those in the mid-level category are described as artists with growing influence, and mainstream category musicians have had steady success across various platforms. The Chartmetric superstar category includes well-known hitmakers and concert draws

Of all artists making music in 2023, 99.9 percent are categorized as either undiscovered or developing. The remaining 0.1 percent are considered mid-level or superstar.

such as Taylor Swift, Bad Bunny, Rihanna, and Kendrick Lamar. The sixth category, legendary, includes artists such as Paul McCartney, Bruce Springsteen, and Bob Dylan, whose careers have lasted more than thirty years.

According to Chartmetric's *Year in Music* report, 99.9 percent of the artists making music in 2023 fell into the two lowest categories: developing and undiscovered. The remaining 0.1 percent, or 10,000 out of 10 million, were labeled as mid-level or superstar. The report did contain some good news: around 12 percent of those in the bottom categories were able to move into the mid-level category. Half of those managed to make it into the mainstream category.

Aim High

Musicians in the undiscovered category might scoff at the complaints made by Prince, Megan Thee Stallion, and other famous artists. Whatever their legal troubles, these superstars get to play

Music Industry Scammers

Struggling musicians who post their music on online platforms such as TikTok, Snapchat, and SoundCloud make tempting targets for scammers. One of the most popular music scams is known as the ex-bigwig scam. Scammers will contact musicians and falsely claim that they are consultants who once worked for a major record label. These supposedly ex-bigwigs will promise the musicians that they can help them get an audition or a record contract. However, the musicians must first pay a fee, which can range from several hundred to several thousand dollars. The scammers disappear once the money is paid, and the musicians are left with nothing.

Another common music industry scam is known as pay-to-play scam. Scammers will promise musicians auditions in front of celebrity judges, A&R directors, or music company executives. But the artists must first pay a hefty performance fee. Another swindle involves a phony talent agency. Musicians are promised gigs if they simply pay a fee for a promo package or demo recording. Industry experts say musicians should never pay for auditions or performance opportunities. As with any business interaction with strangers, proceed with extreme caution.

their music to adoring fans while breathing the rarefied air of the rich and famous. But fighting legal battles against multinational corporations can take an emotional toll on an artist, as British rapper Nadia Rose understands. After her label prevented her from releasing new music in 2020, Rose told an interviewer that it "was one of the most heart wrenching feelings I've ever experienced. I had severe depression. . . . God, family [and] therapy saved me."[46]

> **"As much as [record executives] tell you that they love you, and they'll tell you that you're the next greatest thing, . . . ultimately, they're not your friends."[47]**
>
> **—Bruno Mars, singer, songwriter, musician**

Many musicians play for the love of music, and some dream of sharing their talents with millions of others. While it might be disheartening to delve into the reality of the music business, knowledge is power. Young artists should always consult with their own lawyers before signing any contracts. And they need to understand that they are going up against record companies that have been taking advantage of artists in the same ways for decades. In 2020 Bruno Mars, who was fighting to regain rights to his master recordings at the time, explained the reality of the music business:

> When you sign a contract, you are signing yourself into becoming a commodity. You're becoming a product, and you should understand that. . . . As much as they'll tell you that they love you, and they'll tell you that you're the next greatest thing, ultimately, there's an Excel spreadsheet somewhere with an incoming and an outgoing column, and if that is not balanced and in the green [showing profit], ultimately, they're not your friends.[47]

Mars is one of the lucky superstars who does not need a record company to be his friend. In 2025 he won his sixteenth Grammy Award, this one for his duet with Lady Gaga on the song "Die with a Smile." Mars is an example of someone who came up through the music industry and rose to the top. And his success shows that those who possess talent and drive can overcome industry obstacles and achieve their dreams while aiming for the stars.

SOURCE NOTES

Introduction: Stepping Stones to Success

1. Quoted in Ethan Varian, "Norman's Rare Guitars in Tarzana Rides a Social Media Wave as Six-String Market Shifts," *Los Angeles Daily News*, June 3, 2019. www.dailynews.com.
2. Rich Redmond and Jennifer Della'Zanna, *Making It in Country Music: An Insider's Look at the Industry.* Lanham, MD: Rowman & Littlefield, 2023, p. 7.
3. Redmond and Della'Zanna, *Making It in Country Music*, p. 7.

Chapter One: Music Industry Players

4. Quoted in Leor Galil, "Jon-Carlo Manzo, Indie Tastemaker," *Chicago Reader*, April 18, 2024. https://chicagoreader.com.
5. Quoted in Galil, "Jon-Carlo Manzo, Indie Tastemaker."
6. Quoted in Rania Aniftos, "*Billboard* Explains: What Role Do Record Labels Play?," *Billboard,* March 31, 2023. www.billboard.com.
7. Quoted in Marty Dodson, "Sony Records A&R Director Taylor Lindsey," SongTown, October 31, 2023. https://songtown.com.
8. David Mellor, "The Role of the A&R Manager—What Does He Actually Do?," *Adventures in Audio* (blog), Audio Masterclass, August 28, 2006. www.audiomasterclass.com.
9. Alex Segal, "A Day in the Life of a Talent Agent . . . (plus the Five Essentials That Help My Productivity!)," *Dealmakers with Alex Segal* (blog), InterTalent, April 9, 2024. https://intertalent.substack.com.
10. Quoted in Vincent Jackson, "From the Archives: Stone Harbor Teen Taylor Swift on Her Way to Country Music Stardom," *Press of Atlantic City*, November 20, 2023. https://pressofatlanticcity.com.
11. Quoted in Ray Waddell, "Louis Messina 50th Anniversary Special: The Pollstar Interview," Pollstar, November 7, 2022. https://news.pollstar.com.
12. Quoted in Careers in Music, "Concert Promoter," February 29, 2024. www.careersinmusic.com.
13. Quoted in Careers in Music, "Concert Promoter."
14. Quoted in Careers in Music, "Concert Promoter."
15. Redmond and Della'Zanna, *Making It in Country Music*, p. 22.

Chapter Two: Getting in the Game

16. Elizabeth Gilbert, *Big Magic: Creative Living Beyond Fear.* New York: Riverhead, 2015, p. 12.
17. Quoted in Mark C. Samples, "There's Nothing in Success," *Mark C. Samples* (blog), April 22, 2024. www.mark-samples.com.
18. Redmond and Della'Zanna, *Making It in Country Music*, p. 15.
19. Mathilde Neu, "The Importance of Networking in Music," Reprtoir, August 28, 2023. www.reprtoir.com.
20. Neu, "The Importance of Networking in Music."
21. Kari Estrin, "Three Common Unrealistic Expectations for Musicians," International Acoustic Music Awards, July 19, 2022. https://inacoustic.com.
22. Redmond and Della'Zanna, *Making It in Country Music*, p. 19.

Chapter Three: Making Money from Music

23. Quoted in *CanvasRebel*, "Meet Jason Blume," December 19, 2022. https://canvasrebel.com.
24. Quoted in *American Songwriter*, "Artists Relate How Partnership with DistroKid Platform Is Empowering Music Innovation," January 9, 2025. https://americansongwriter.com.
25. Laura Simpson, "Turn One Gig into 10—Making Your Audience into Venues," *Bandzoogle Blog*, August 25, 2022. https://bandzoogle.com.
26. Quoted in Gili Malinsky, "This Musician Makes $4,500 a Month Streaming Her Songwriting Process on Twitch," CNBC, February 20, 2021. www.cnbc.com.
27. Quoted in Clifford Thurlow, "Bob Dylan's Secrets of Success," Medium, November 15, 2020. https://medium.com.

Chapter Four: How Stars Are Born

28. Quoted in Lizzy Goodman, "Kendrick Lamar, Hip-Hop's Newest Old-School Star," *New York Times*, June 25, 2014. www.nytimes.com.
29. Quoted in Andrew Noz, "Black Hippy: A View from the Center—Kendrick Lamar," *The Fader*, February 20, 2012. www.thefader.com.
30. Quoted in Noz, "Black Hippy."
31. Quoted in Steve Appleford, "The Rebel Girls of the Linda Lindas," *Spin*, October 17, 2024. www.spin.com.
32. Quoted in Appleford, "The Rebel Girls of the Linda Lindas."

33. Quoted in Cece Mitchell, "The Linda Lindas Are 'Growing Up' with 'No Obligation,'" Iowa Public Radio, October 30, 2024. www.iowapublicradio.org.
34. Quoted in Chris Azzopardi, "An Interview with Chappell Roan, Who Is Being Called the 'Queer Pop Moment,'" QBurgh, November 12, 2023. https://qburgh.com.
35. Quoted in Tamia Fowlkes, "'Midwest Princess' Chappell Roan Talks Queerness, Girlhood, and Growing Up," *Milwaukee Journal Sentinel*, October 4, 2023. www.jsonline.com.
36. Quoted in Ellise Shafer, "Confessions of a 'Midwest Princess': How Chappell Roan's Debut Album Arose from the 'Deep Pits of Hell' to Become a 'Dream Come True,'" *Variety*, September 22, 2023. https://variety.com.
37. Quoted in Shafer, "Confessions of a 'Midwest Princess.'"
38. Quoted in Shafer, "Confessions of a 'Midwest Princess.'"
39. Quoted in Ryan Reed, "Kendrick Lamar Wins Pulitzer Prize for Music," *Rolling Stone*, April 16, 2018. www.rollingstone.com.

Chapter Five: Reality Check

40. Lisa Kay Davis, "Prince Fought Big Labels for Ownership, Artistic Control," NBC News, April 11, 2016. www.nbcnews.com.
41. Quoted in Lynn Norment, "The Artist Formerly Known as Prince," *Ebony*, January 1997, p. 128.
42. Circa, "5 Reasons You Should Never Sign a Major Label Record Deal," Indepreneur, August 24, 2022. https://staging.indepreneur.io.
43. Quoted in Mark Savage, "From Prince to Megan Thee Stallion: When Record Contracts Go Wrong," British Broadcasting Corporation, March 3, 2020. www.bbc.com.
44. Aryan, "Unveiling the Dark Side of the Music Industry: Exploitation, Mental Health, and Challenges," Medium, August 16, 2023. https://medium.com.
45. Greg Fuhs, "How Spotify Is Stealing from Small Indie Artists, Why It Matters, and What to Do About It," *Indie on the Move* (blog), March 12, 2024. www.indieonthemove.com.
46. Quoted in Savage, "From Prince to Megan Thee Stallion."
47. Quoted in AWAL, "Why Owning Your Master Recordings Means Everything." www.awal.com.

FOR FURTHER RESEARCH

Books

Jeff Chang and Dave Cook, *Can't Stop Won't Stop (Young Adult Edition): A Hip-Hop History*. New York: Wednesday 2021.

Thomas Deerborn, *From Song to Streaming: 7 Step Roadmap for Publishing Your Music on the World's Biggest Platforms.* Self-published, 2025.

Sinead O'Sullivan, *Good Ideas and Power Moves: Ten Lessons for Success from Taylor Swift*. New York: Viking, 2025.

Rich Redmond and Jennifer Della'Zanna, *Making It in Country Music: An Insider's Look at the Industry*. Lanham, MD: Rowman & Littlefield, 2023.

Mason Young, *So You Want to Be a Musician: A Real Life Guide for Creating a Life as a Musician*. Self-published, 2024.

Internet Sources

Rania Aniftos, "*Billboard* Explains: What Role Do Record Labels Play?," *Billboard*, March 31, 2023. www.billboard.com.

Chris Azzopardi, "An Interview with Chappell Roan, Who Is Being Called the 'Queer Pop Moment,'" QBurgh, November 12, 2023. https://qburgh.com.

Circa, "5 Reasons You Should Never Sign a Major Label Record Deal," Indepreneur, August 24, 2022. https://staging.indepreneur.io.

Mathilde Neu, "The Importance of Networking in Music," Reprtoir, August 28, 2023. www.reprtoir.com.

Laura Simpson, "Turn One Gig into 10—Making Your Audience into Venues," *Bandzoogle Blog*, August 25, 2022. https://bandzoogle.com.

Ethan Varian, "Norman's Rare Guitars in Tarzana Rides a Social Media Wave as Six-String Market Shifts," *Los Angeles Daily News*, June 3, 2019. www.dailynews.com.

Websites

American Guild of Music (AGM)
www.americanguild.org
This organization is open to musicians, music teachers, music publishers, instrument makers, and students. The AGM sponsors music contests, concerts, teacher workshops, and traveling displays of musical instruments and music.

Bandzoogle
https://bandzoogle.com
The stated goal of this website is to empower artists to build good websites for their music. But the platform also offers dozens of informative blogs about marketing, songwriting, and other topics useful to up-and-coming musicians.

Careers in Music
www.careersinmusic.com
This website features articles with career advice, listings of music schools, industry contacts, and occupations that can be pursued by a professional musician.

Majoring in Music
www.majoringinmusic.com
Majoring in Music is aimed at those who are searching for music schools, summer music programs, scholarships, and other information needed to make smart decisions about establishing a sustainable musical career.

Youth Music Project
www.youthmusicproject.org
This Oregon-based organization is dedicated to providing rock, pop, and country music education to young people. The project offers a high school intern program, tuition assistance, instrument use, and a stage for performance opportunities.

INDEX

Note: Boldface page numbers indicate illustrations.

PICTURE CREDITS

Cover: LightField Studios/Shutterstock

6: Sayre Berman/Alamy Stock Photo
10: Mo Photography Berlin/Shutterstock
13: ShotPrime Studio/Shutterstock
14: Associated Press
19: Paul Froggatt/Shutterstock
21: Krakenimages.com/Shutterstock
25: PintoArt/Shutterstock
28: GBJSTOCK/Shuttertock
30: ssi11/Shutterstock
33: Roman Voloshyn/Shutterstock
37: David Buono/Icon Sportswire DCV/David Buono/Icon Sportswire/Newscom
40: CraSH/ZUMAPRESS/Newscom
42: L Paul Mann/Shutterstock
47: Anthony Correia/Shutterstock
50: sirtravelalot/Shutterstock
53: AnnaStills/Shutterstock

ABOUT THE AUTHOR

Stuart A. Kallen is the author of more than 350 nonfiction books for children and young adults. He has written on topics ranging from the theory of relativity to the art of electronic dance music. In 2018, Kallen won a Green Earth book award from the Nature Generation environmental organization. He has also written award-winning children's videos and television scripts. In his spare time, he is a singer, songwriter, and guitarist in San Diego.